SELF-PUBLISH YOUR MEMOIR OR FAMILY HISTORY

BEVERLEY EIKLI

Copyright © 2023 by Beverley Eikli

All rights reserved.

No part of this book may be reproduced in any form or by any electronic or mechanical means, including information storage and retrieval systems, without written permission from the author, except for the use of brief quotations in a book review.

❦ Created with Vellum

About the Author

Beverley Eikli teaches family history and memoir, writing, and self-publishing.

She also writes historical fiction and historical romance as Beverley Oakley, and Africa-set romantic suspense as B. G. Nettelton.

After the rights to her first five traditionally published novels reverted to her, she began her self-publishing journey.

She has now published 40 titles.

The second half of this book outlines her process.

Find out more at www.beverleysbooks.com

Contact her at: beverley@beverleysbooks.com

Contents

Introduction	vii
Family History - Getting Everyone on Board	1
Use Technology to Fast-track your Family History	4
Family History Questions	17
Genealogy Tools and Services	26
Different Family Tree Layouts	29
30 Prompts for Memoir and Family History	34
Memoir: Narrative Arc and Flow	38
Different Approaches to Writing a Memoir	42
Considerations for Writing A Memoir	44
Using the Senses	47
Writing as Therapy	49
Tips for Polishing and Editing your work	52
Steps to Self-publish	55
Outsourcing the Components of your Project	62
From Ring-binder to Published Book - Example	79
Useful Resources and Software	89

Introduction

What is the difference between a Memoir and a Family History?

Why could this Guide be Useful to me?

Family History

A family history is a record of a family and of the lives of family members.

Throughout the following chapters, I offer ideas for organising and recording a family history. I also provide useful technology tips to streamline the process.

Memoir

A memoir is an entirely personal account. It's authored from the perspective of an individual, recounting a significant part of their

Introduction

life with a firm grounding in factual events. Unlike an autobiography that encompasses the writer's entire life journey up to the present, a memoir concentrates on a specific period or theme.

In the following chapters, I'll suggest options to frame and structure your memoir, starting with useful prompts, and then outlining different popular approaches.

Self-publishing in ebook and print-on-demand

The final part of this book outlines the step-by-step process I use—with photographs—to turn a written Word or text document into a format suitable for e-readers or print books.

I also show you how you can make your book accessible world-wide (at local shipping costs) for little more than the cost of a couple of tickets to the movies!

I hope you discover invaluable tools within these pages to make your work-in-progress or "book of the heart" a more manageable and satisfying experience.

Beverley Eikli

Family History - Getting Everyone on Board

So you're going to start your Family History project?

The prospect of delving into boxes of photos and letters can be daunting.

Where will you start?
What will you include?
How will you structure it?

Wouldn't it be nice to have other family members to help?

Here are some ideas to get others onboard, and to spark their enthusiasm with a sense of purpose.

Share the Benefits:
Emphasise the significance and long-lasting impact of preserving family history. Explain how writing the family history can provide a sense of identity, connection to roots, and a legacy for future generations. Highlight the value of passing down stories, traditions, and memories to create a stronger family bond.

Start Small:

Encourage individuals to start with manageable tasks. Break down the process into smaller, achievable steps, such as organising photos, selecting a few meaningful letters, or focusing on a specific time period. By starting small, it becomes less overwhelming, and progress can be made gradually.

Personalise the Approach:

Have a family get-together to brainstorm different angles or perspectives for approaching the family history. Explore specific themes, such as immigration, family traditions, or notable achievements. By personalising the project, it becomes more engaging and meaningful.

Provide Inspiration:

Share success stories or examples of published family histories to inspire and motivate family members. Show them how others have navigated the process and produced beautiful and compelling narratives. Sharing inspiring anecdotes and the positive impact of preserving family history can fuel enthusiasm.

Collaborative Approach:

Suggest that other family members take a specific role in the process. By turning it into a collaborative effort, you'll share the workload, exchange memories and stories, and strengthen family bonds. Encourage them to reach out to relatives for their input, contributions, and support.

Utilise Technology:

Introduce tools and resources that can simplify the process.

Digital platforms, genealogy software, or online family history websites can help individuals organise, digitise, and preserve photos, letters, and documents. Highlight the convenience and accessibility that technology offers in capturing and sharing family history.

Break the Ice with Prompts:

Check out the thought-provoking prompts or questions provided in later chapters of this book, and also in the Self-publish your Family History or Memoir spiral-bound workbook that is designed to accompany this how-to volume.

Questions and prompts can tap into a mine of information that can be directly recorded. (See the chapter on Use *Technology to Fast-track your Family History*.)

Questions and prompts can also kickstart the writing process for a memoir by sparking memories and inspiring storytelling.

Celebrate Achievements:

Recognise and celebrate milestones and accomplishments along the way. Acknowledge the efforts and progress made by individuals. Establish mini-goals or rewards to keep the enthusiasm and motivation alive throughout the process of putting together your family history.

Offer Support and Guidance:

Be available to provide guidance, answer questions, or offer assistance when needed. Suggest regular family get-togethers to review work or progress, provide feedback, or help with organising materials. This can alleviate concerns and boost enthusiasm.

The key is to make the process approachable, meaningful, and rewarding, igniting everyone's passion for preserving the legacy of their family.

Use Technology to Fast-track your Family History

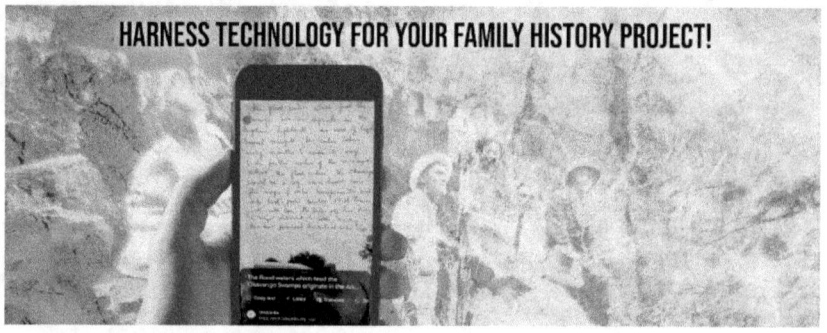

One of the most daunting aspects of putting together a family history is collating and digitising old letters, documents and photographs.

Here are some Apps and tools I use and recommend.

. . .

Please note: *I am not affiliated with any organisation, apps or software mentioned in this chapter, and earn no commission.*

Simple (free) voice-to-text technology through email

Getting the whole family involved not only shares the load but can be a great way to forge new connections with family members.

Conversations between generations can unlock a treasure-trove of memories; and using the simple voice-to-text functionality built into a smartphone's operating system, or through downloadable applications, can be a great way to do this.

Speech-to-text—also sometimes referred to as voice-to-text or voice recognition—allows users to convert spoken words into text, making it easier to compose messages, emails, notes, and other text-based content without typing manually.

I specifically chose my Pixel 6—several years ago—due to the speed and accuracy of its Assistant Voice typing capacity.

Check if *your* smart phone is set up to recognise voice typing. If it is, you might have to explore how to turn it on.

Record conversation using voice-to-text to save typing out transcripts.

Even young children can record the answers to simple questions by putting a smart phone near the person speaking.

. . .

If the mobile phone is set to record from voice to text directly into the phone's email app, the question and response can be emailed or shared.

It might take a little practise to get the sequence of question and answer right, but it's a direct, easy way of producing editable text instantly to your email or wherever else you want to share it.

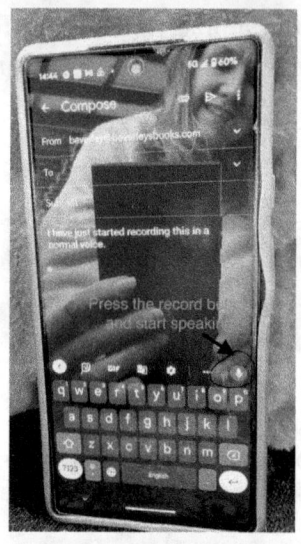

My Pixel 6 is a couple of years old but the dictation function is very accurate.

Voice-to-text functionality has become increasingly common across mobile platforms, including Android and iOS.

It is, however, important to note that the availability and performance of voice-to-text may vary depending on the specific device model, software version, and language settings.

Here's how I do it using my mobile phone

- Step 1: Open Gmail on my Pixel 6 Android mobile.
- Step 2: Press 'compose message'.
- Step 3: Press the microphone icon on the bottom right to instantly record.
- Step 4: When finished speaking, press send to the recipient of the email (usually myself).

I now have the transcript to incorporate into my manuscript.

Alternatively you could send it to the family member in charge of collating the interview.

Sometimes I send it to Google Docs as I have Google Docs on my mobile phone and synced to my computer.

If you use Gmail, Google Docs is a great central repository for information from everyone involved in your family history project.

Collaboration using Google Docs

Google Docs can be shared with anyone you choose via an emailed invitation. This makes it a great way of gathering all family material —interviews, etc —in the one place.

And, of course, now the conversation or interview, or photographed text, is editable, it can be moved around the word document of the first draft of a family history.

Using the voice-to-text app on your computer

More recent models of computers and laptops have an excellent dictation function these days.

On an MacBook Air, this is how to access it:

Place the insertion point where you want the dictated text to appear. If available in the row of function keys, use the dictation keyboard shortcut, or choose Edit > Start Dictation. to activate Siri. (Siri must be enabled).

The shortcut is simply to press the Function key (FN) key, twice.

No Need to Transcribe Handwritten letters

Here's a paragraph of text I photographed from my father's annotated photo album.

Google Lens

Google Lens if my favourite App for streamlining my family history project.

. . .

It can:

- Convert photographed text into editable text.
- Transcribe handwritten letters into editable text. And,
- It can translate text from hundreds of languages - both in print and handwriting.

Google Lens is a free app which I've installed on my Pixel 6, an Android mobile which is several years old. It's very easy to instal and use but there's a slightly different process if you are using an Apple iPhone.

Android: On Android phones, you can install the Google Lens app from the Play Store, use it inside Google Photos or use the Google Lens icon in your Google Assistant.

Apple: Google does not provide a dedicated Google Lens app for iOS. However, you can install the Google app on your iOS device and tap the Lens icon to open Google Lens.

Copy-Paste Text From Textbooks and Documents

Google Lens' ability to copy-paste text enables a fast, accurate way to copy from a document, into your own document. Its OCR (Optical Character Recognition) allows you to read any character from an image and turn it into editable text.

I've used it, below, to photograph a page from my grandpa's diary, then, using Google Lens, email it to myself.

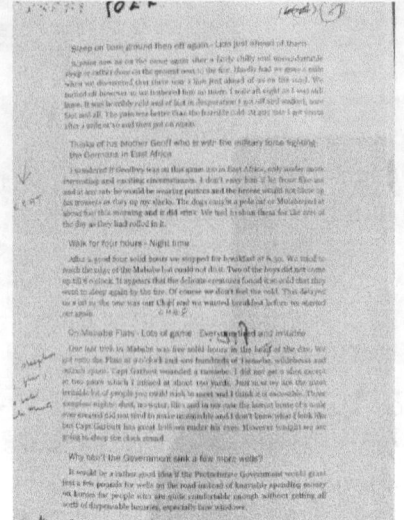 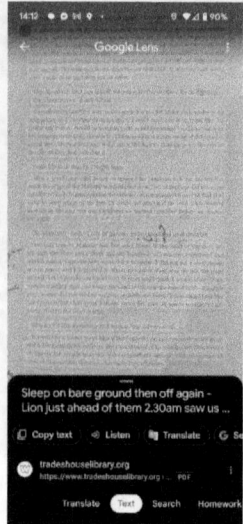

On the left is the photograph I took on my mobile phone. Even in a bad light, Google Lens recognised the text, as you can see from the highlighted text on the right.

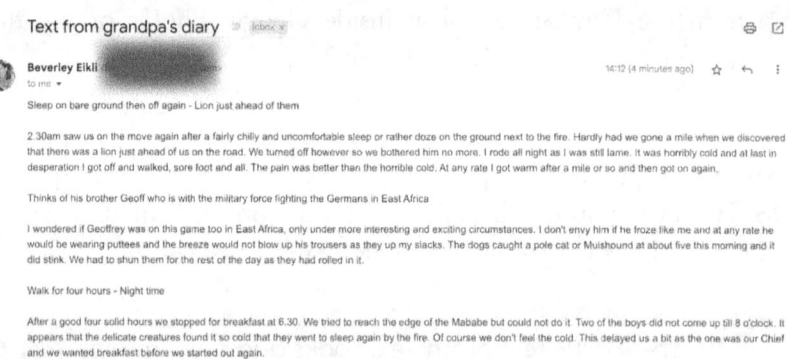

After pressing copy text (example, top right), then email, this is the unedited transcription I received. Very accurate!

Digitise handwriting

As an example of how I can turn handwriting into a digitised format, as well as scan and edit photographs, I've used a page of my father's photograph album from a visit we took together to Botswana in 1992.

I wanted to digitise all the information—photographs and captions—so I could incorporate it into the single Word file I'm using to collate the family history.

Using two of my favourite apps—**Google Lens** and **Photomyne**—I was able to do this in minutes.

Here's a photo of the album's page with its separate components that will be scanned using my mobile phone.

You'll note that my father's handwriting in the following example isn't the easiest to read, however I was delighted by the accuracy of Google Lens's transcription.

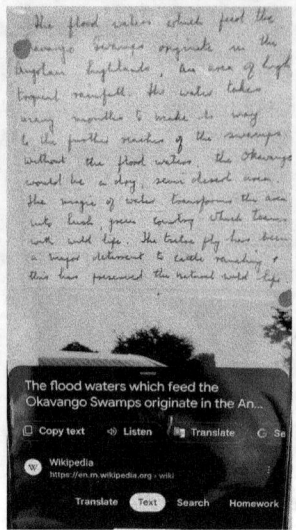

Below are several ways to copy-paste text using the Google Lens app:

1. Open the Google Lens app (These instructions are for Android.)
   2. Point your phone's camera over all the text you want to scan (so it is all highlighted).

Tap on the **Text** icon.

Tap on **Select All** (or you can tap on sections of text you want to select).

Tap on **Copy text**.

Open up the app or document you wish to copy the text into (I use Google Docs or gmail on my phone).
   7. Long press the cursor in your document to summon the

selection menu.

Tap **Paste**.

Transcribe handwriting using your mobile or within you photos on your desktop or laptop or tablet.

You can use Google Lens on a mobile phone or tablet to identify any objects in your phone's camera.

As it searches for the objects, it recognises text .

Open the Google Lens app on your mobile phone. **On an iOS device, tap the Lens icon in the Google app.**

Step 1. Open your camera

Step 2. Point the phone or tablet's camera over the **hand-written notes**.

Step 3. Select the text you want.

Step 4. Press 'select all' (or 'Listen' if you want it to play back).

Step 5. Press 'copy text'

Step 6. Press the 'share' icon to share it to wherever you'd like it to go.

This could be to your email, or Google Docs, or a PC associated with your Google account. The text is **copied to the clipboard** on the PC.

Here's how to copy-paste text using the Google Lens icon inside the Google Photos app on your computer:

1. Open **Google Photos**.
    2. Open the photo you want to copy-paste text from.
    3. Tap in the **Google Lens** icon

Need translation? Use the same free App!

Google Lens also supports translation.

. . .

You can even transcribe letters written in a foreign language.

Simply, place the camera over the writing to be translated - text or handwriting—press select—then press translate.

Use Google Translate to translate a Conversation

What if a child and grandparent don't speak the same language?

Google Translate on your iPhone or Android is a great way to get the conversation going.

Google Translate is a free translation app for iPhone and Android.

It offers over a hundred language choices and can translate handwriting, voice, text and photos taken with your phone's camera.

In a real-time conversational setting, it will detect both chosen languages, turn everything into text, and then an automated voice will translate between the two speakers.

It's as simple as pressing the record button to speak and then another button to hear the translation.

Photos

I use the Photomyne App to scan old photograph albums in a hurry.
    A feature I enjoy is the colouration feature.

Below is a picture of my grandparents on their wedding day in Botswana in 1926.

Photomyne can instantly colourise old black and white or sepia photographs. Of course we don't want all our old black and white photos in colour but in some cases, the flesh tone and colours can make our forebears seem closer to us.

Black and white photo of my grandparents' wedding

Photomyne is one of many apps to help digitise your photos and slides but I've included its many features here because I find it fast and easy and it includes the following:

FilmBox leverages the Photomyne scanning software to convert negatives into photos you can share with family and friends and/or save in albums on your smartphone. This particular app also allows you to add corresponding details to keep your memories fresh.

In addition to Filmbox, Photomyne also offers 7 other apps to turn all your physical slides and film memories into digital gems:

• **LifeShow** – If you like creating slideshows, this app will help you animate them, providing the transitions necessary to keep the past alive.

• **FridgeArt** – Clear the clutter from your fridge by digitizing your child's art with FridgeArt.

• **SlideScan** – Use this tool to take photo slides from your smartphone and convert them to digital photos.

• **Colorize** – This app lets you turn black and white photos into color after scanning/uploading them. Give new life to the past with the Colorize app.

• **Photo Family Tree** – Build your family tree by uploading family portraits. Photo Family Tree will automatically recognise your relatives to assign pictures accordingly. It can even score you against your family members to see how similar you really look.

• **Face / Face** – How much do you resemble your family members? Score your similarity with this app.

• **FamilyStars** – Looking for a dynamic way to make memories? Complete challenges with your family and friends to build a one-of-a-kind photo album you can cherish for years to come with FamilyStars.

Photomyne front screen

So, now that you have a few handy Apps and software to choose from that can make your task easier, the following chapter offers some handy prompts to launch into your project.

Family History Questions

1. What is your name?

2. When were you born/ and where?

3. Did your birth take place in a hospital, at home?

4. Was there a doctor or midwife present?

5. Did you have siblings?

6. What are their names and when were they born?

Conversation starters

1. Is there an interesting story about your birth?

2. Did you get along with your siblings?

3. Did you have any animals or pets growing up?

4. What's your earliest memory?

5. Was there some special adult in your life?

6. What was your biggest adventure?

7. What was your biggest disappointment?

8. What was your biggest achievement?

9. What special skills did you have?

10. How did you meet your husband/wife/partner?

Discovering more about the next generation information

1. What is your mother's full name/date of birth? Where was she born?

2. What is your father's full name/date of birth? Where was he born?

3. What did your father do for a living? Did he have more than one profession?

4. What kind of work did your mother do? Was she employed outside the home?

5. Describe your memories of your mother from growing up.

. . .

6.   Describe your memories of your father from growing up?

7.   What important life lessons did your parents teach you?

8.   Did your parents have any friends that had a big influence on you?

9.   What family activities did you enjoy most?

10. How would you describe the parenting style of your parents? Strict? Loving? Were both parenting styles the same?

Basic information about Grandparents and great-grandparents

1.   What were your maternal grandparents' names and dates of birth? Where were they born?

2.   What were your paternal grandparents' names and dates of birth? Where were they born?

3.   What kind of work did your grandparents do?

4.   Where did your maternal grandparents live?

5.   Where did your paternal grandparents live?

. . .

6. Do you have special memories of your grandparents?

7. What food did you have when you visited?

8. Did you do any special activities?

9. Are you named after one of them? And if so, why?

10. If they died before you knew them, how are they remembered?

Childhood - School and Home

1. Did you go to school or were you home schooled?

2. How did you get to school?

3. Did your school have a uniform?

4. Who was your favourite/most influential teacher? Why?

5. Who was your least favourite teacher? Why?

6. What were your favourite subjects? Your least favourite?

7. Were you good at anything in particular at school or home?

. . .

8. What were the most important skills that you learned at home?

9. What kind of clothing did you wear? Was it homemade?

10. Did you have a special occasion dress or outfit?

Special occasions

1. What was your favourite holiday or special occasion?

2. How were birthdays celebrated in your family?

3. What's a special memory from a birthday, Christmas or special occasion?

4. Was your family religious? What place of worship did you attend?

5. How did you celebrate special holidays? Did you give gifts, decorate, dress up, go to church or worship?

Your teenage years

1. How many years of school did you attend?

2. Did you do an apprenticeship, go to TAFE, college or university? Where, when? What did you study?

. . .

3. What were your goals, hopes, and dreams as a young adult?

4. What was your first job? How old were you?

5. Did you have more than one job? Which was the best? Why? What were the people you worked with like?

Older years

1. What was/is your occupation/trade? Have you had multiple professions over the years?

2. What tasks did your work involve? Did you enjoy the work?

3. If you could have chosen another profession, what would it have been?

4. Did you ever get married?

5. When, where, and how did you meet your spouse?

6. How did you get engaged?

7. What was your wedding like? What did you wear, what food was served, where was it held?

8. Who were your bridesmaids/best man?

9. Did you go on a trip or honeymoon after the wedding? Where to?

10. If you chose not to marry, what was the reason?

About your partner/spouse

1. What is your spouse's full name? Their siblings and parents?

2. What is your spouse's occupation? Interests?

3. Can you describe a little about your spouse's personality?

4. What do you love the most about your spouse?

5. What was your first home together like? Where was it? Did you rent it, buy it?

6. What would you say is the key to a successful marriage?

7. Do you have any children? How many?

8. What are the names and birth dates of your children? The names of their spouses?

9. Do you remember what it was like finding out you would soon be a parent?

10. What were your children's births like? At the hospital, at home? Who was there?

11. What city or county were each of your children born in?

12. Where did you live when your kids were growing up?

13. Did you move around much? Why did you move and to where?

14. What was your home(s) like when your children were young? Did you own or rent?

15. What special memories do you have of your children's baby or preschool years?

16. What was your favourite way to spend time with your kids?

17. What was the most difficult part of raising kids? The best part?

18. What hobbies did you have when you weren't working or caring for children?

19. What kind of music did you like to listen to?

20. What kind of books/magazines did you like to read?

Travel and World Events

1. How many nationalities/passports do you have?

2. How many places have you lived? Travelled to?

3. Which was your favourite?

4. Which did you dislike the most? Why?

5. What major world events have happened in your lifetime? Did any have a big effect on you?

7. Which personal events in your life would you say had the greatest impact on you?

8. What's the best advice you can give your great-grandchildren, your great-great-grandchildren?

10. What do you want people to remember the most about you?

Genealogy Tools and Services

A genealogy society can offer a range of tools and services to individuals researching their family history. Check out the ones near you, though these are some common offerings:

Research Resources: Genealogy societies often provide access to a variety of research resources. This can include physical libraries or archives with books, periodicals, manuscripts, maps, and other historical records relevant to genealogical research. They may also offer online databases, subscriptions to genealogical websites, and access to specialised software for organising and analysing family tree data.

Expertise and Guidance:
Genealogy societies often have experienced researchers and volunteers who can provide guidance and support. They may offer consultations or workshops to help beginners get started, provide

advice on research techniques, and assist in navigating challenging aspects of genealogical research such as deciphering old handwriting or understanding complex historical contexts.

Educational Programs: Societies often organise educational programs such as lectures, workshops, and seminars. These events can cover a wide range of topics, including research methodologies, DNA testing, understanding historical documents, preserving family artefacts, and more.

Online Communities and Forums: Many genealogy societies maintain online communities and forums where researchers can connect with fellow enthusiasts, ask questions, share information, and seek advice. These platforms often foster a supportive and collaborative environment, allowing individuals to connect with others who share their interests and potentially discover relatives or connections they were previously unaware of.

Publications and Newsletters: Genealogy societies might publish newsletters or magazines with articles, case studies, research tips, and updates on the latest genealogical resources and techniques. These publications provide valuable insights, research methodologies, and news about upcoming events or opportunities within the genealogy community.

Local and Regional Research Assistance: Genealogy societies often have a focus on a specific region or locality. They can provide specialised knowledge about local history, archives, and resources that may be relevant to researchers in that area. This includes information on local cemeteries, historical societies, local government records, and other regional repositories.

· · ·

Collaboration and Networking: Genealogy societies can facilitate collaboration and networking among researchers. They may organise conferences, conventions, or local meetups where individuals can share their research, connect with others who have common ancestors or interests, and learn from experienced genealogists.

It's important to note that the services and tools provided by genealogy societies may vary. It's advisable to research and reach out to the specific society you are interested in to understand their offerings in detail.

Different Family Tree Layouts

Below are a variety of different formats and layouts of Family Trees.

Which is the best way of setting out your family history?

1. **Traditional Book Format:** This format involves writing a narrative-style family history book. It may include chapters for each generation, individual family members' stories, historical context, and relevant photographs. Family trees can be interspersed throughout the book or placed in separate sections.

2. **Descendant Chart:** A descendant chart shows the direct lineage of a specific ancestor, starting from them and going down (or up) through their descendants over multiple generations.

The family tree of Louis III, Duke of Württemberg (ruled 1568–1593)

You could get colourful and creative like the above example.

3.   Pedigree Chart: A pedigree chart starts with a specific individual and traces their lineage back through multiple generations, showcasing their ancestors.

Self-publish your Memoir or Family History

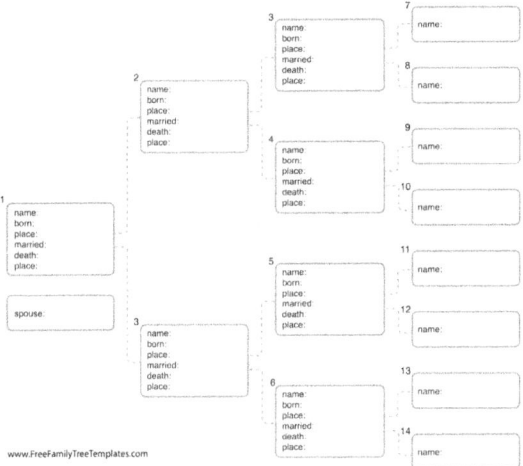

There are many sites where you can download ancestor charts that can fit the date of birth, birthplace, marriage date, death date, and place of death. Download this one at: https://freefamilytreetemplates.com/4-generation-ancestor-chart/

4.   Fan Chart: Fan charts are visually appealing and show a person or couple at the center, with their ancestors fanning out in different generations. This format provides a compact overview of multiple generations.

Birth Country

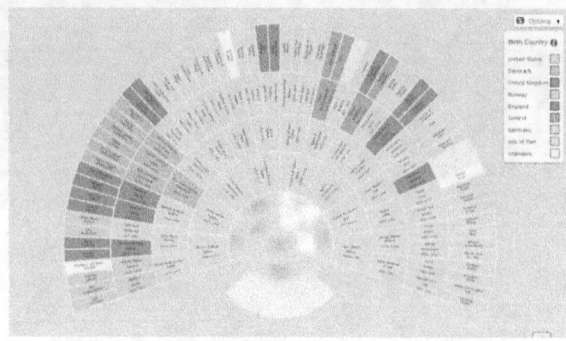

The FamilySearch Family Tree provides an easy, free family tree template for your genealogy. Not only do you have four options for viewing your online family tree chart, but you can also print and display your genealogy fan chart in seven ways. See: FamilySearch.org

5.   Interactive Online Family Trees: Utilize genealogy websites or family tree software to create interactive online family trees that can be easily shared and collaborated on by family members.

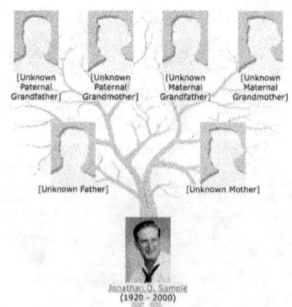

This is one of many examples from Wikitree which has downloadable templates: https://www.wikitree.com/printable/family-tree-diagram.html

6.   Collage or Scrapbook Format: Create a visual family history using photographs, documents, and memorabilia arranged creatively in a scrapbook or collage format.

7. Multimedia Presentation: Combine photos, videos, and audio recordings to create a multimedia presentation that brings your family history to life.

8. Digital Family History Website: Build a dedicated website to showcase your family history, including family trees, stories, photos, and historical documents.

The format you choose will depend on your objectives, the amount of information you have, and your creative vision for presenting your family history. Whether it's a printed book, online tree, or multimedia project, your goal is to preserve and share your family's heritage for generations to come.

30 Prompts for Memoir and Family History

1. Describe a pivotal moment from your childhood that shaped who you are today.

2. Reflect on a significant relationship in your life and the impact it had on you.

3. Recount a challenging obstacle or setback you faced and how you overcame it.

4. Share a humorous or lighthearted anecdote that brings a smile to your face.

5. Explore a period of personal growth or transformation and the lessons you learned.

. . .

6. Discuss a cherished family tradition or ritual and its significance to you.

7. Describe a place that holds deep meaning for you and the memories associated with it.

8. Reflect on a major life decision you made and the reasons behind it.

9. Recall a memorable trip or adventure that left a lasting impression on you.

10. Share a story of resilience and perseverance in the face of adversity.

11. Discuss a passion or hobby that has shaped your life and brought you joy.

12. Reflect on your experiences with self-discovery and personal identity.

13. Explore the theme of forgiveness and reconciliation in your life.

14. Discuss the role of faith or spirituality in your journey and how it has influenced you.

. . .

15. Reflect on your relationship with your parents or grandparents and the lessons they taught you.

16. Recount a significant event from history that had a profound impact on you personally.

17. Discuss your experiences with love, heartbreak, or navigating romantic relationships.

18. Reflect on a time when you had to make a difficult ethical or moral choice.

19. Share a story of personal triumph or accomplishment that made you proud.

20. Discuss your aspirations for the future and the legacy you hope to leave behind.

21. What is the earliest memory you have of a family member, and what stands out about it?

22. Are there any unique or interesting family traditions that have been passed down through the generations? Can you describe them?

23. Can you share any stories or anecdotes about our ancestors that have been told within our family?

. . .

24. Are there any significant historical events or milestones that our family has witnessed or been a part of?

25. What were the occupations or professions of our ancestors, and did any of them have notable achievements in their fields?

26. Are there any family recipes or culinary traditions that have been handed down? Could you share one of your favorites?

27. Can you recall any family legends, myths, or rumors that have been circulating throughout the generations? What do you know about them?

28. Were there any challenges or hardships that our ancestors faced, and how did they overcome them?

29. Are there any cultural or ethnic traditions that our family has maintained over time? Can you provide some insight into their significance?

30. What are some memorable family gatherings, reunions, or celebrations that you recall? What made them special or unique?

Memoir: Narrative Arc and Flow

When mapping your journey and creating a structured narrative arc for your memoir, consider the following strategies:

Identify Key Moments:
Reflect on your life experiences and identify the key moments, events, or themes that shaped your story. These could be pivotal turning points, significant relationships, personal achievements, or challenges you've overcome.

Select the most compelling and relevant moments to serve as the foundation of your narrative.

Establish a Clear Beginning:
Start your memoir with a compelling opening that hooks the reader and sets the stage for your story. Consider beginning with a vivid memory, an impactful event, or a powerful statement that

grabs the reader's attention and introduces the central theme or conflict of your memoir.

Determine the Narrative Flow:

Decide on the chronological or non-linear structure of your memoir. Chronological order follows a timeline from the beginning to the end, while a non-linear structure may involve flashbacks, reflections, or thematic chapters. Choose a structure that best suits your story and effectively conveys the intended emotional impact.

Build Tension and Conflict:

Introduce conflicts, obstacles, or challenges that you faced along your journey. Show the emotional, physical, or psychological struggles you encountered and how you navigated your way through them. Build tension by highlighting the stakes involved and the impact of these conflicts on your personal growth or transformation.

Show Transformation and Growth:

Illustrate how you changed, grew, or evolved throughout your journey. Demonstrate the lessons learned, insights gained, and the impact of your experiences on your identity or worldview. Capture the emotional and psychological shifts that occurred and highlight the significance of these transformations.

Use Scenes and Dialogue:

Bring your memoir to life by incorporating vivid scenes and authentic dialogue. Show, rather than tell, your experiences, allowing readers to immerse themselves in the moments. Use sensory details, descriptions, and engaging dialogue to create a rich and immersive reading experience.

Remember to incorporate *all* senses. For example: Describe the smell of baking bread during visits to your grandparents; or the cold, harsh wind on your cheek if they lived by the sea.

Connect Themes and Motifs:

Identify overarching themes, motifs, or recurring symbols throughout your memoir. These can be used to create cohesion and provide a deeper layer of meaning to your narrative. Weave these themes and motifs into different sections of your memoir to create a sense of unity and resonance.

Maintain a Balance:

Balance the intensity of emotional moments with lighter or reflective passages. Vary the pacing of your memoir to provide moments of reflection, humour, or contemplation amidst more intense or dramatic scenes. This balance keeps the reader engaged and creates a dynamic reading experience.

Consider Chapter Endings:

Craft compelling chapter endings that leave the reader wanting more. End each chapter with a sense of anticipation or a question that encourages readers to continue on the journey. This keeps the momentum of your narrative and ensures readers are eager to dive into the next chapter.

Mapping your journey and creating a structured narrative arc is a dynamic process. Continually revise, refine, and reshape your memoir as you progress, ensuring the narrative arc remains coherent, engaging, and impactful.

Tip! Don't over-revise before a good portion - if not, all, of your first draft is complete.

. . .

Editing and layering your narrative:

When I've finished my rough draft, it's time to let the work 'sit' for a while in order to gain the necessary distance needed to identify where additions could be made, or where 'less is more.'

'Layering' is the term I use to add sensory detail.

Writing tips to increase tension

Adjusting the pacing, flow and sentence structure of your narrative at certain points makes for a more interesting reading experience.

One way to do this is to imagine you're filming the scene. Concentrate on the small, telling details as you progress towards whatever is the conflict or climax of your story.

This is the place to use more descriptive language.

When you've reached the climax of your story, use short, sharp sentences to create a sense of urgency in the reader to know now.

Turn off your Internal Editor and write from the heart!

Remember that you are writing this memoir from your perspective and from the heart.

It is inevitable that a rough draft will be just that - rough!

Therefore be forgiving of yourself as you craft what might be a difficult to write from an emotional perspective.

The polishing and reshaping process will take time.

No one will see your manuscript until you want them to.

Therefore, don't be constrained about what others might think of the way you've told a story, or what a disapproving relative might think.

The magic comes in the polishing.

And that can only happen after you have thrown everything you have at the page in a first **rough** draft.

Different Approaches to Writing a Memoir

There are various approaches you can take depending on your personal style, goals, and the story you want to tell.

Here are five to consider:

Chronological Approach: This is the most traditional and common approach to writing a memoir. You start from the beginning and move forward in a linear fashion, recounting events and experiences in the order they occurred. This approach allows readers to follow your journey and understand how you've evolved over time.

Thematic Approach: Instead of following a strict chronological structure, you can organise your memoir around specific themes or topics. For example, you could choose to focus on your relationships, career, or personal growth. Each chapter or section can explore different aspects of your life, providing a deeper exploration of the chosen theme.

Event-Based Approach: With this approach, you centre your memoir around significant events or milestones that have shaped your life. These events could be joyful, challenging, or transformative. By delving into these key moments, you provide readers with a clear narrative arc and a focused exploration of pivotal experiences.

Geographic Approach: If your life has involved various locations or a strong connection to a particular place, you can structure your memoir around different geographical settings. This approach allows you to explore the impact of these locations on your life, culture, and identity. Each setting becomes a backdrop for the stories and memories you wish to share.

Hybrid Approach: You can also combine different approaches to create a unique structure for your memoir. For example, you could use a chronological framework but include thematic chapters or employ an event-based structure with geographical sections.

The key is to find a structure that best serves your story and allows you to present your experiences in a compelling and coherent manner.

Remember, these approaches are not mutually exclusive, and you can adapt and combine them as per your needs. The goal is to find a structure that resonates with your story and helps you communicate your experiences effectively to your readers.

Considerations for Writing A Memoir

Writing a memoir involves sharing personal experiences and insights, often including the people who have been a part of your life. When considering the people you're writing about in your memoir, here are some suggestions to keep in mind:

Respect privacy: Be mindful of the privacy and feelings of the individuals you're writing about. Consider changing or omitting names, altering identifying details, or seeking permission from the people involved before sharing personal information. Respect their boundaries and ensure that their privacy is protected.

Reflect on your intentions: Ask yourself why you are including certain individuals in your memoir. Is it essential to the story? Does it contribute to the overall message or theme? Avoid including people simply for shock value or to settle personal scores. Be thoughtful about your intentions and the impact your words may have on others.

Seek consent: If possible, reach out to the individuals you plan to write about and discuss your intentions with them. Seek their consent to include their stories or experiences in your memoir. This dialogue can help you understand their perspectives, address any concerns, and establish open communication.

Maintain empathy and compassion: Remember that the people you write about are complex individuals with their own emotions, experiences, and perspectives. Approach their portrayal with empathy and compassion. Try to present them as multidimensional characters rather than one-dimensional stereotypes. Show understanding and avoid unnecessary judgment.

Be honest and authentic: Authenticity is crucial in memoir writing. Share your experiences truthfully and genuinely, including both positive and negative aspects of the people you write about. However, be aware of the potential impact your words might have on their reputation or relationships. Be honest without being hurtful or unnecessarily invasive.

Consider different viewpoints: Acknowledge that memory can be subjective, and others may have different recollections of events. Be open to alternative perspectives and consider incorporating them into your narrative. This shows respect for multiple viewpoints and promotes a well-rounded depiction of the people in your memoir.

Consult a legal professional if necessary: In some cases, you might have legal considerations when writing about real people, especially if your memoir includes sensitive or potentially damaging information. Consult a legal professional to ensure that you navigate any legal boundaries or risks associated with your writing.

Remember, striking a balance between sharing your truth and respecting the privacy and feelings of others is crucial in writing a memoir.

By being mindful of the people you write about and approaching their portrayal with sensitivity, you can create a memoir that is both authentic *and* considerate.

Using the Senses

Engaging the senses can add depth and richness to your writing, allowing readers to connect more deeply with the story.

Here are ten ways to use the senses in writing your memoir or family history:

Sight: Describe the visual aspects of places, events, and people. Use vivid imagery to paint a picture in the reader's mind, helping them see the world through your eyes.

Sound: Incorporate sounds, such as the laughter of family gatherings, the clinking of dishes, or the rustling of leaves, to create an immersive atmosphere.

. . .

Taste: Share memorable food experiences, the flavours of traditional dishes, or unique recipes passed down through generations.

Smell: Explore the aromas associated with certain places or moments, like the scent of a childhood home, freshly baked bread, or the fragrance of flowers in the garden.

Touch: Describe tactile sensations, such as the feeling of soft fabric, the roughness of an old family heirloom, or the warmth of a loved one's hand.

Emotions: Connect sensory experiences to emotions, expressing how certain sights, sounds, tastes, smells, or touches evoked specific feelings and memories.

Seasonal Changes: Use the changing seasons as a backdrop for your stories, describing how they influenced family traditions or the mood of different occasions.

Family Rituals: Describe family rituals and customs that involve the senses, such as holiday traditions, storytelling around a campfire, or gatherings with specific themes.

Writing as Therapy

Writing your story can be a powerful form of self-expression and self-healing. Here are several ways in which writing can be used as therapy:

Self-Reflection: Writing allows you to explore and reflect on your thoughts, emotions, and experiences in a safe and private space. It encourages you to dig deep into your feelings and gain a better understanding of yourself.

Emotional Release: Putting emotions into words can be cathartic. Writing about painful or traumatic experiences can help you release pent-up feelings and create a sense of emotional relief.

Validation and Empowerment: Through writing, you can validate your own experiences and feelings. By acknowledging your struggles and triumphs, you can empower yourself to overcome challenges and grow stronger.

Processing Trauma: Writing about traumatic events can be part of the healing process. It allows you to confront and make sense of what happened, gradually reducing the emotional impact over time.

Gaining Perspective: Writing your story can provide you with a different perspective on your life and experiences. It can help you see patterns, recognise strengths, and identify areas where you want to make positive changes.

Stress Reduction: Engaging in creative writing can be relaxing and reduce stress. It shifts your focus away from daily worries and allows you to immerse yourself in the therapeutic process.

Building Resilience: Sharing your story on paper allows you to see how you've overcome challenges in the past. This can boost your confidence and resilience, reminding you of your ability to handle difficulties.

Creating a Narrative: Writing your story helps create a coherent narrative of your life. It can give you a sense of continuity and purpose, even during times of uncertainty.

Sense of Accomplishment: Completing a written piece, whether it's a memoir, journal entry, or creative story, can give you a sense of accomplishment and pride.

. . .

Connecting with Others: Sharing your writing, whether with a therapist, support group, or loved ones, can foster connections and a sense of community. It allows others to understand your experiences and offer support.

Reclaiming Your Voice: For some individuals, writing can be a way to reclaim their voice, especially if they've experienced silencing or marginalisation in their lives.

It's important to note that while writing can be therapeutic, it is not a substitute for professional mental health care. If you're dealing with significant emotional challenges or trauma, consider seeking support from a trained therapist or counsellor who can provide guidance and expertise in navigating these experiences.

Writing can complement therapeutic work and be an additional tool in your healing journey.

Tips for Polishing and Editing your work

Polishing and editing your work is an essential part of the writing process. Here are some suggestions to help you polish and edit your writing:

Take a break: After finishing your first draft, set it aside for a while. Taking a break allows you to approach your work with fresh eyes and a clear mind.

Read aloud: Read your work aloud to yourself. This helps you identify awkward sentence structures, grammatical errors, and areas that need improvement. It also helps you gauge the flow and rhythm of your writing.

Focus on clarity and coherence: Ensure that your ideas are communicated clearly. Look for any confusing or convoluted sentences and rephrase them to enhance clarity. Ensure that your paragraphs flow logically from one to another, creating a cohesive and coherent piece.

Once I am happy with the structure of my work as a whole, it's time to return to the specifics of the writing.

For this, I utilise my favourite free editing software—Pro-writing Aid—which I'll talk about in greater depth in a following chapter. I paste my work into the programme so it can pick up typos, grammar mistakes, and suggest improvements to sentences which I can either accept or dismiss. Its suggestions can help with the following:

Cut unnecessary words and phrases: Eliminate wordiness and streamline your writing. Look for redundant words, clichés, and excessive adjectives or adverbs. Keep your sentences concise and to the point.

Check grammar, spelling, and punctuation: Pay close attention to grammar, spelling, and punctuation errors. Use spelling and grammar check tools, but don't rely solely on them. Proofread your work manually to catch any errors that might have been missed.

Vary sentence structure: Aim for sentence variety to maintain reader engagement. Alternate between short and long sentences, simple and complex structures, and vary your sentence beginnings to create a more dynamic writing style.

Develop strong transitions: Smooth transitions between paragraphs and ideas improve the overall flow of your writing. Use transitional words and phrases to connect thoughts and guide the reader through your work.

Seek feedback: Share your work with others, such as writing groups, friends, or trusted colleagues. Their fresh perspectives can provide valuable insights and constructive criticism to help you identify areas for improvement.

Consider the reader's perspective: Put yourself in the reader's shoes and evaluate your work from their standpoint. Is the information presented clearly? Are the ideas organised in a logical manner? Does the writing engage and hold their interest?

Revise and repeat: Editing is an iterative process. After making the necessary changes, revise your work again. Repeat this process until you are satisfied with the final result.

Remember, editing and polishing take time and effort, but they are essential for transforming your initial draft into a polished, refined piece of writing.

Steps to Self-publish

- **Write your story, memoir or family history**
- **Edit it**
- **Format it; and**
- **Publish it!**

These are the most basic steps required, but with so many options at each turn, it can be confusing to choose the best path for *you*.

Writing options

Some people write straight into Microsoft Word, others prefer Scrivener or other software to help organise their chapters.

Previous chapters in this book have detailed the writing process, but when you are happy with your manuscript and ready to publish, where do you go from there?

Publishing options

1. You can shop it around to find a traditional publisher.

2. You can pay a company to edit, format, publish (and, perhaps) market it for you.

3. You can do it all yourself (which requires a lot to learn).

Or - my preferred method -

4. You can outsource each different component—ie, editing, formatting, cover design, publishing—to different professionals while retaining overall control, much like you would project-manage a building project or kitchen renovation.

The positives and negatives of the traditional approach vs the do-it-yourself (Indie- or self-publishing) approach.

Pros of Signing with a Traditional Publisher:

Professional Editing and Production:
Traditional publishers typically have a team of professional editors, proofreaders, and designers who work on your book. They can help improve the quality of your writing, ensure proper formatting, and create an attractive cover design.

Distribution and Marketing Support:
Traditional publishers have established distribution channels and relationships with bookstores, online retailers, and libraries. They can help get your book into physical and digital stores, increasing its visibility and accessibility to readers. Additionally, they often provide

marketing support, including promotional campaigns, author events, and media exposure.

Credibility and Prestige:
Being published by a traditional publishing house can bring a level of credibility and prestige to your work. It is often seen as a validation of the quality and marketability of your writing, which can help build your reputation as an author.

Advance and Royalties:
Traditional publishers may offer an advance payment to authors, which serves as an upfront payment before the book is published. Additionally, authors typically receive royalties based on book sales, allowing them to earn ongoing income from their work.

Drawbacks of signing with a traditional publisher

Limited Control:
When signing with a traditional publisher, authors may have to relinquish some control over their work. Publishers may have the final say on aspects such as editing, cover design, and title. The author's creative vision may not align completely with the publisher's decisions.

Longer Time to Publication:
The traditional publishing process can be lengthy, involving several stages such as manuscript review, editing, production, and marketing. It may take years from the time of signing a contract to the actual release of the book.

Lower Royalties:
While traditional publishers offer advances and royalties, the

percentage of royalties received by authors is often lower compared to self-publishing. This is because the publisher takes a significant share of the revenue to cover their costs, including editing, printing, marketing, and distribution.

Limited Acceptance and Competition:
  Traditional publishers receive a vast number of submissions and can only accept a limited number of books each year. The competition to secure a publishing deal can be fierce, and many authors may face rejection or struggle to capture the attention of publishers.

  Ultimately, the decision to sign with a traditional publisher depends on the individual author's goals, preferences, and circumstances. It is essential to carefully weigh these pros and cons, consider the specific terms and conditions of any publishing contract, and assess how well they align with your long-term writing and publishing objectives.

Pros and cons of paying a company to edit, format, publish and market for you.

If you don't go the traditionally published route but you don't have the energy or interest in self-publishing, then you might choose to pay someone, or a company, to do this for you.

Be careful. My biggest advice is to shop around and, if preferable, get word-of-mouth recommendations if you plan to hand your manuscript over to a publishing company to whom you will *pay* money, rather than who will pay *you*.

Look at the reviews about a company to whom you might be paying hundreds—of not thousands—of dollars to edit, format, and publish your work. The actual process of getting you work into print is not costly. (I will go through the costs of editing, cover design, and formatting in a later chapter.)

Find out where their greatest costs lie? Are they promising advertising and promotional support? Remember that there can be no guarantees for the results of this support.

So, check online reviews, or through a writers' organisation like the Alliance of Independent Authors (ALLi), a non-profit professional association for authors who self-publish. They have a global team who provide trusted, best-practice information and advice to the author community. Their Ask Alli forum answers any question anyone might have about self-publishing.

While getting someone else to publish your book may be the ideal option for you, make sure they are a good fit.

Due Your Due Diligence and be Wary of Scams

Novice writers who are eager to see their work in print can be vulnerable to scams when it comes to self-publishing or vanity publishing companies.

Unscrupulous entities prey on the dreams and aspirations of aspiring authors. One common scam is the promise of quick and easy publication, coupled with exorbitant fees.

Novices may be enticed by the allure of becoming a published author without fully understanding the publishing industry or the necessary steps involved. Scammers may charge authors hefty upfront fees for services such as editing, cover design, formatting, and marketing, without delivering on their promises or providing quality results. As a result, novice writers can end up spending a significant amount of money with little or no return on their investment.

Another scam tactic is the lack of transparency in contractual agreements. Some publishing companies may manipulate authors into signing complex contracts that include unfair terms, such as high royalty deductions, extended rights ownership, or hidden fees. Novice writers, unfamiliar with industry standards and legal intricacies, may unwittingly sign away their rights or fall victim to exploitative clauses.

Furthermore, these unscrupulous companies often lack proper distribution channels and marketing strategies, making it difficult for authors to reach their intended audience and generate sales. This can lead to frustration, disappointment, and financial loss for inexperienced writers who were hoping for a legitimate publishing opportunity.

To avoid falling into these scams, it's crucial for novice writers to conduct thorough research, seek advice from reputable author communities or writing organisations, and carefully scrutinise any publishing agreements before committing their time, money, and intellectual property.

So, before making any binding agreements with a company to publish your work, check their reputation and ensure that they are reputable. The Alliance of Independent Authors is an organisation that can help you with this.

. . .

You may find the perfect partner to whom to hand over your work, and who will then produce a beautiful book. I've listed several in the Useful Resources and Software Chapter.

If they ask for extra money to market it, be careful about what you agree to. You may decide you simply want them to produce the book which you can then upload to the retailers, retaining full control from that point onwards.

Choosing the Self-publishing Option and doing it yourself!

In the next chapter I'll go through the steps I use to go from finished manuscript to publishing my book in print and as an ebook.

Outsourcing the Components of your Project

This can seem more complicated than it is, largely because some of the steps need to be completed before others—if you are choosing one option over another.

For example, if I do my own formatting, I need to know the number of pages first, in order to inform the professional cover designer I've commissioned.

However, if I choose to build my own cover using some of the tools within, for example Amazon's KDP or Ingram Spark, I don't need a wraparound cover, and therefore I can make changes to my manuscript without it having an impact on the cover.

Outsourcing the individual components is my preferred method as it offers me the most control for the cheapest price.

What 'parts' can you outsource?

- Editing
- Cover
- Formatting your manuscript
- Uploading the correct files
- Printing

You've done the hard, time-consuming work of writing your Memoir or Family History. Now that you have finished it, you should feel very proud of what you've achieved!

Getting a Word manuscript from your computer and into print or ebook can seem daunting.

Let's go through the above, one by one.

Editing

You should always get someone to edit your work. You are too close to the words to get the big picture or to pick up the typos.

Below are options for editing:

1. Have a fellow writer/writer's group look at it. You want the story to be structurally sound. Or…

2. Find an editor to give it a structural edit. (An 80K manuscript might cost AUD400 to $1000 or $1500.)

3. You might not need a structural edit. A line edit/proofread might be sufficient.

Be aware that there are different types of editing.

A structural edit is 'big picture' editing.

A line/copy edit is like proofreading.

After I've decided that I'm happy with the structure and 'big picture' aspects of my work, I will put the manuscript through Pro-Writing Aid, which is software designed to pick up errors, and that suggests better writing, at the grammatical and typo stage.

You can get a free version of this here:
https://prowritingaid.com/

Here are some of Pro Writing Aid's features:

It can help shorten sentences, ditch weak adverbs, and add sensory details to any sentence instantly.

It's a great method of fixing common first draft issues and frustrations.

It can eliminate surface errors like overlooked typos, punctuation errors, extra spaces, and grammar issues with a quick scan.

It can shorten sentences if you choose to adopt their suggestions, remove jargon, and make your tone more formal or conversational, depending on your audience.

Tip! I use Pro-writing Aid so I can deliver the cleanest manuscript to my outsourced editor. That means they are not distracted by typos and bad grammar and can concentrate on things like structure and narrative arc.

Formatting

Formatting and uploading to the retailers costs little time and expense. As I mentioned earlier, you could outsource your manuscript in the same way you might project manage the building of a house or refurbishing of a kitchen. You will have control over which particular tiler, painter, stonemason, etc, you contract for the job.

Formatting is necessary to get the file formats you need for:

- Ebooks – (which requires an .epub)
- Print – (which requires two PDFs—one PDF for the interior, and one PDF for the cover).

How do you format your manuscript?

To format your file, two options I recommend are:

1. Vellum if you have a Mac. (https://vellum.pub/)
2. D2D (Draft2Digital) https://www.draft2digital.com/faq/

OR:

Outsource it to a formatter. This is a quick job and you should get it done for around $100.

I suggest you look for 'Book Formatter' on https://www.fiverr.com/ or at reedsy.com.

First, let me talk briefly about these two platforms which I have found so useful in my journey from writing the book to getting it into the world.

What is Fiverr?

Fiverr is a multinational online marketplace for freelance services. Fiverr's platform connects freelancers to people or businesses looking to hire. Listings on Fiverr are diverse and range from "get a well-designed business card" or "help with HTML, JavaScript, CSS, and jQuer" or "Find a Cover Designer" and "Find a Formatter".

What is Reedsy?

Reedsy is a platform that allows you to connect with designers, editors, translators, and marketers who have extensive experience in the publishing space.

Reedsy has freelancers for just about every step of the publishing process: there are editors and designers, translators, book marketers, website designers, book marketers, book reviewers, and even book publicists. Reedsy launched in November of 2014, making it an experienced and well-rounded marketplace.

Currently, there are over 150,000 authors who are using the platform. However, unlike most other freelancer platforms, every freelancer who receives an account is **vetted by the Reedsy team** to verify they perform their service at the highest level quality.

Now, back to the process of self-publishing ...

Once the interior of your book is formatted, you will need a book cover.

For an ebook, you only need the front cover. Sizing the cover for an ebook is not as important as getting the sizing exactly right for a print book.

When you upload your files to get your book into print, print-on-demand publishers like Amazon, Ingram Spark, D2D, Lulu, etc, will give you the option to use your ebook cover as the front cover while you 'build' the back cover and spine, according to the trim size of your book, and the width of the spine.

You could make your own cover using Canva, Bookbrush (designed for writers), or PicMonkey.

For an ebook, I only need the front cover

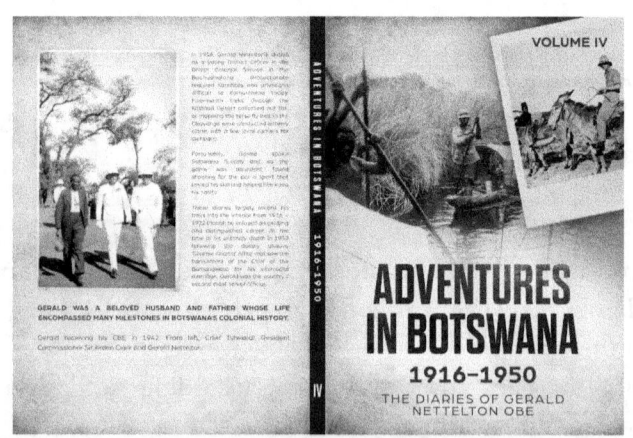

For a print book, the wraparound cover needs to incorporate the spine. (The spine width is dependent upon the number of pages.)

My preference is to have a professional cover designer make me a wraparound cover.

For one of my book series, I use Fiverr.com (and pay between AUD$45 and $100 per cover).

For another series, I use a US cover designer who understands the requirements of the historical romance genre in which I write. She was a word-of-mouth recommendation who makes many covers for genre writers.

What Information do you need to provide your cover designer when making a paperback book?

- Trim Size
- No. of pages
- Paper (cream or white)

Generally, fiction is printed on cream paper, while non-fiction is printed on white paper.

The cover designer needs to know whether white or cream paper is used because 100 pages of cream paper will result in a different spine width compared with 100 pages of white paper.

Use the Ingram Spark Template to produce the cover size to give to your designer

Alternatively, you can generate a template once you've uploaded your book's basic details. Then you'd simply email that to your cover designer. It's what I usually do. (More on this, later.)

. . .

Once you have your cover back from the designer as a .PDF, you'll upload that, plus the interior .pdf file, to Ingram Spark or your chosen print-on-demand service or publisher.

Formatting the book yourself

This will need to be completed before you can get a wraparound cover sized correctly, because, as mentioned, the number of pages (and trim) will determine the exact dimensions.

Another option for formatting yourself is to use Draft2Digital (D2D) – which is a multi-function platform.

This is a great option if you have a Word document as you can have it formatted at no cost.

D2D will:

Format your eBook AND your print book.

It will also distribute your books to the retailers **IF YOU CHOOSE**.

However, at no cost, you can feed in your Word file, and it will turn this into an .epub to upload it as an ebook, or .pdf which you will need if you plan to publish in print.

With these files, you are free to upload to the retail or printing or publishing platform of your choice.

. . .

So, now that your book has been edited and formatted, what now?

PRINT

I use Ingram Spark for my print books because they have printers in Australia, as well as worldwide.

That means that if my book is being bought by someone in, for example, the UK, they will only pay local shipping because it will be printed at the closest local printer – on demand.

This makes it a cost-effective option for distribution, whether it is being acquired by a family member overseas, or a reader to whom I have sold my book.

Other print-on-demand services include Lulu, Bookvault and Amazon. (These are the ones I use though there are many more.)

How to do it using Ingram Spark:

You can upload your two .pdf files to Ingram Spark (https://www.ingramspark.com/) and they will print and distribute it.

It's a good option for people who want small amounts of Print on Demand (POD) copies for family and friends.

You can set it to private or if you want to make it available commercially, and market to libraries and the public at large, just set it to public.

On the below websites, you can prepare your book as both an ebook or a print book.

Here are the websites which will outline the specific instructions for doing either or both.

https://draft2digital.com/

https://www.ingramspark.com/

https://kdp.amazon.com/en_US/

Whichever sites you are going to use, you will have to set up a free account first.

Then, if you want a print book, you will need two files:

- Interior
- Cover

Ingram Spark will require two already formatted .pdf files.

D2D is simpler as you can use a word .doc file for the interior.

Note!

For the above printers, you don't *need* a single wraparound cover for your print book as they provide the tools to help you 'build' your own cover in three parts: Front, Spine, and Back.

However, I choose to outsource a complete wraparound cover to my cover designer because I have no design talent while I know my cover designer will provide something much more professional than I could ever produce—and at a reasonable cost.

What do I need to Upload? At the risk of sounding repetitive, I'll say it again:

For Ingram Spark you will need:

- A formatted .pdf for the interior.
- A wraparound .pdf for the cover based on the number of pages of your interior.

Tip! The size of the cover of a print book will change with the addition of just a few pages as this alters the width of the spine for a wraparound cover.

Other useful Sites for Cover Design & Formatting

For formatting, I use Vellum for a .pdf interior.

https://vellum.pub/ (This is for Mac only)

https://www.fiverr.com/ A freelancer site that offers formatting, design, and many other related options

https://reedsy.com/ - A great, curated site for finding editors, formatters, cover designers, etc

And for DIY design, Canva, PicMonkey, and BookBrush are great.

https://www.canva.com/en_au/
https://bookbrush.com/
https://www.picmonkey.com/

Below are some helpful hints from the respective site's Frequently Asked Questions Pages.

Draft2Digital - Formatting, Publishing & Distribution

Below are some of the frequently asked questions answered by D2D about their site and services.

D2D charges nothing to use their tools. There are no costs associated with using them to format your book and generate the files you need to upload to any print-on-demand service.

However, if you choose to distribute to the retailers through them, they will take a small percentage of each sale.

What do I need to make a Draft2Digital account?

It is free to make an account with Draft2Digital. All you need to sign up is a name and an email address that you can check regularly. We will keep the name on your account separate from any Pen Names. There is no upfront cost to using Draft2Digital.

Can you really turn my manuscript into a book?

Yes! Draft2Digital offers ebook and print book publishing services. If you have a complete story or manuscript, D2D can convert your work into a beautiful electronic book (ebook) or print on demand (POD) paperback book.

As a self-published author, you are the publisher of your own books and you retain the intellectual property rights of your story. You control when and where Draft2Digital sends your book.

Even if you choose not to publish with us, we have you covered. Draft2Digital gives you the option of downloading the files we convert for you at no charge. You can create, convert, and download a pixel-perfect paperback PDF or ebook EPUB file without having to publish through D2D.

What file types can Draft2Digital take and make?

The most popular file format that authors upload is a Word document. Upload your book in .doc or .docx file format, and we'll convert your manuscript into an ebook or print book. Anything Word can read, we can read. (RTF, OTF, TXT, too!)

If you already have an epub of your own, Draft2Digital accepts epub files for ebook, but not print. We won't make any changes to your epub formatting, but we'll gladly distribute it to all our digital stores for you.

What file types will Draft2Digital NOT accept?

We do not accept printed manuscripts; Draft2Digital can only convert electronic file types. Because of the fixed nature of PDFs, Draft2Digital cannot convert PDFs to any other file type. PDFs are only accepted as print book interior or print book cover files.

Where's your style guide?

Our goal is to support *your* writing without you having to worry about formatting. As such, we accept a variety of document formatting styles and don't have any single style guide.

If you'd like some direction on creating a simple style that will convert beautifully every time, do these two things:

• Skip the title page, copyright page, dedication, also by, about the author, teaser, and any biographical pages. *You only have to upload your story.* Let us help you add the technical stuff later.

• Mark each new chapter or scene break with something distinctive, *and **be consistent***. Make new chapter titles centered and bold, or larger font, or use a heading style. The most important part is to do the same thing to each chapter title or scene break so that our system can learn your style.

That's enough for our tools to build a beautiful ebook out of your manuscript.

This all sounds great, but it's an automated system. What if there are problems with my book?

We've got you covered. Draft2Digital is famous for our friendly and knowledgeable customer support.

Ingram Spark

Ingram Spark talks about the following in their Frequently Asked Questions:

Editing

Some editors charge per word, some charge per page, and some charge per hour. The <u>**Editorial Freelancer Association**</u> provides rough guidelines to give you an idea of common editorial rates. (Note that these are US dollars.)

Developmental Editing (estimated pace 1-5 ms pgs/hr): US$45-55/hr

Substantive or Line Edit (estimated pace 1-6 ms pgs/hr): $40-60/hr

Basic Copyediting (estimated pace 5-10 ms pgs/hr): $30-40/hr

Proofreading (estimated pace 5-10 ms pgs/hr): $30-40/hr

When you're ready to hire an editor, do some research and request a few different quotes. Meet with them, if possible, or have a conversation to get to know whether or not they'll be the best editor for your book's content. Have they edited in that genre before? Do you feel like they understand your writing style? Ask them for references or examples of their work to make the most informed decision.

ISBNs

One publishing expense you'll incur is purchasing an ISBN, if you choose not to use a free ISBN. This is necessary if you'd like to enable your book for distribution, and each format of each book you publish must have its own unique ISBN.

As part of our catalog integrity initiative, we require that ISBNs are valid and properly acquired. Each country has a single approved and designated agency that issues ISBNs for publishers and self-publishers located in that country. Bowker is the official ISBN agency for the US; Nielsen is the official ISBN agency for the UK and Ireland; Thorpe-Bowker is the official ISBN agency for Australia. IngramSpark does business in many other countries, so we encourage each customer to ensure they are acquiring their ISBN from their country's approved ISBN Agency. You can find the approved ISBN agency for your country on the International ISBN Agency's Website.

For U.S. customers, ISBNs can be purchased from Bowker directly through your IngramSpark account for $85 each. You can also buy a block of ten ISBNs from Bowker for $295. At Ingram-Spark, we believe it's in your best interest to be recognized as the owner of your work and a publisher in your own right, which is why we encourage publishers to purchase their own ISBNs.

If you want your book to be available in brick-and-mortar bookstores, you'll need a barcode in addition to your ISBN. Some ISBN services sell barcodes, as well as ISBNs, but you can use Ingram-Spark's book cover template generator to get a free barcode.

Printing & Shipping

The cost to print and ship a book with IngramSpark depends on the following:

- Trim Size
- Interior Colour and Paper
- Binding Type (paperback or hardback)
- Laminate Type (gloss, matte, or textured)
- Page Count
- Quantity
- Ship-To Address

IngramSpark has a **Print and Ship Calculator** to help you understand how much it will cost.

From Ring-binder to Published Book - Example

As a final wrap-up or overview of the process from start to finish, I've used my grandfather's collection of photographs, typed diary, and other documents to show you how I turn it into a published ebook and paperback.

Here is it, collated in a spiral-bound folder.

My father did the time-consuming job of selecting what would go into his final three volumes of memoirs.

My job was as editor, formatter, and publisher.

Let's get started!

Front cover of my grandfather Gerald Nettelton's Botswana diary

I wanted to create one word document with the text.

I also wanted to include photographs, maps, newspaper clippings and other items like plane tickets, etc.

. . .

And I wanted to organise the project myself so I could have everything in the right file format to upload to my chosen print-on-demand publisher, Ingram Spark.

Many printers will do minimum print-runs that would require me having boxes of books in the garage which I would have to hand-sell.

I wanted to my book to be available to friends and family all over the world, and for them to be able to access my paperback or hardcover—with colour photographs—for less than a movie ticket or two, and to only pay local shipping.

So, I chose Ingram Spark because they have printers in Australia as well as worldwide.

This required deciding upon the technology that would make the task easier.

My dad's memoirs of his life growing up in Botswana in the 1930s and 40s was originally written as one long narrative starting with the day he was born.

Subsequently, he broke this up in dozens of stories to create two volumes of his own Memoirs as he decided that breaking it up into stories made for a better reading experience.

His forebears would be more interested in dipping in and out—and he was right.

• • •

The previous photograph shows the ring-binder filled with scanned photographs and photocopies letters and other material.

A few years ago this would have taken months—and a great deal of money—to transcribe.

I began the task of digitising everything using Google Lens. It took me a few hours to simply photograph the text to turn it into editable text which I put into one Word file.

I also photographed the photos from the various photo albums.

Using the Photomyne App, this was also a quick task.

I then had one word file, and a number of individual .jpegs which I kept separate. (For formatting purposes, they did not go into the word file which was for text only.)

When I had one single word file (244 pages) plus dozens of separate photographs (.jpeg files), I was ready to format.

But how would I do that?

As dad had three volumes, I chose to outsource both the editing and formatting to local editor Pip Butler, who produced two volumes using InDesign software.

. . .

I liked having someone in the local area with whom to discuss the process, and the layout, and was very happy with the result. Pip provided me with the necessary interior .pdf.

Then, according to the number of pages, she resized the .pdf wraparound cover I'd had designed by my cover designer LesCreative on Fiverr.

I then made my free account on Ingram Spark, then uploaded the two .pdf files—interior and cover.

The next day I received the online proof from Ingram Spark which I approved.

The book was now ready for distribution—worldwide.

Dad's Third Volume - & Formatting it Myself

As I use a Mac computer which is compatible with my favourite formatting software, Vellum, I decided to try formatting his memoirs, including photographs, myself.

How did I do it?

I simply opened Vellum and copied and pasted in the text, chapter by chapter.

This is what Vellum looks as you're working. The right is what the formatted output looks like.

When I wanted to add an image, I just pressed 'Add Image'. It was that easy.

When all my words and images were input and I was happy with my 30+ chapters, and had included the self-generated Copyright page', I simply pressed "Generate".

Generate File

I then chose the 'trim' size I wanted. In this case, it was a 9in x 6in Trade Paperback size.

At the same time, I asked it to generate an .epub which I would use to upload as an ebook.

I now had my formatted:

- .pdf for print books
- .epub for ebooks

Choosing the retailer or print-on-demand service.

I wanted to make dad's memoirs available on Amazon as an ebook plus print book, so I made a free account and followed the prompts.

Ebook — I uploaded my .epub file plus cover
    Print — I uploaded my .pdf interior plus .pdf cover

I then repeated the process, as described earlier, with Ingram Spark.

Again, Ingram Spark generated an online proof within a couple of days, which I checked, approved, and then was able to order a print proof.

And here is the result:

Dad's Memoirs in print

I chose a hardcover version, on the right, and a paperback version, on the left.

The wonderful part about self-publishing it was that I could change the interior file and then republish it, at no added expense other than the single proof copy which was less than a ticket to the movies.

. . .

For example, when we got the proof, other family members wanted to make inclusions.

We then added extra material, I pasted two extra chapters into Vellum, regenerated the file, and I simply uploaded the new .pdf to Ingram Spark and the new .epub file to Amazon's KDP, and to D2D.

Note that while this did not require any changes to the cover of the ebook, it did require changes to the size of the wraparound cover. I had to ask my cover designer to resize the cover to accommodate the extra spine width.

I then uploaded the new cover to Ingram Spark.

And I ordered a new proof.

Dad's memoirs are now out in the world. They are accessible to his relatives, worldwide, and only at the minimal cost of around $25 per copy, plus local shipping, depending on how close the Ingram Spark printer is. (Ingram Spark has printer partners in Germany, India, Italy, Poland, Russia, China, Spain, Brazil, and South Korea.) Therefore, shipping costs are kept to a minimum.

The wonderful part of all this is that if Great-aunt Edna reads dad's memoirs and then divulges her secret life as a spy which is integral to part of dad's family story, then her additions can be included, and the book can be regenerated, at any time, as described above.

. . .

So, there is the process, in a nutshell, of getting your work from an idea into a book you can hold in your hands and which your relatives can enjoy, and to which they can make their own contributions.

I hope you've found something here to help and inspire you.

Happy writing—and happy publishing!

Useful Resources and Software

Here are some useful resources and software that I mention in this guide.

Naturally, these only scratch the surface and there are many more, but these are the ones I have used and can recommend.

Apps for fast-tracking your project

- Google Lens
- Photomyne
- Google Translate

Editing - software and freelance help

- Pro-writing Aid
- Grammarly
- Fiverr or Reedsy (for sourcing a freelance formatter)

Cover Design

- Fiverr or Reedsy (for sourcing a freelance formatter)
- Word-of-mouth
- Canva
- PicMonkey
- BookBrush

Formatting

- Vellum
- D2D (Draft2Digital)
- Fiverr or Reedsy (for sourcing a freelance formatter)

Recommended companies that will hold your hand through the publishing process.

These are simply two (of many reputatable publishing companies) that I've recommended based on the recommendation of author friends.

- Wakefield Press
- Busybird Publishing

Print-on-demand options

- D2D (Draft2Digital)
- Ingram Spark
- Lulu
- Amazon KDP

Genealogy sites. The following was compiled from positive review sites which highlight the following features:

· MyHeritage—Excellent for Global Database and family matching.

· Ancestry—Great for reading through historical records

· FindMyPast— Best For English or Irish Ancestry

· Genes Reunited—Best for English, Irish or Welsh Ancestry

· Legacy Tree Genealogist—Best for hiring trained Genealogists for custom projects

· JustAnswer—Best for research from Experts

Copyright-free images

- unsplash.com
- Free Range
- Pexels

Assistance, resources, advice for self-published Authors

https://www.allianceindependentauthors.org/

Finally, I have created two Workbooks to go with this Self-publish your Family History or Memoir.

One is the spiral-bound **Family History Work Book** filled with numerous prompts and questions, with space for answers.

· · ·

The other is the spiral-bound **Memoir Work Book** filled with numerous prompts and questions, with space for answers.

Everyone will find their own way of putting together their family history or memoir.

All the best with your project. I hope some of these ideas have been helpful.

You can buy the accompanying workbooks, and find out more at www.beverleysbooks.com

Get the eBook version of Write and Self-Publish Your Memoir or Family History for FREE when you buy the paperback.

Scan the QR code to get your free ebook – when you buy the paperback – using the code: MyBook